Editor
Kim Fields

Managing Editor
Ina Massler Levin, M.A.

Editor-in-Chief
Sharon Coan, M.S. Ed.

Illustrator
Kelly McMahon

Cover Artist
Denise Bauer

Art Coordinator
Kevin Barnes

Imaging
Temo Parra

Product Manager
Phil Garcia

Publishers
Rachelle Cracchiolo, M.S. Ed.
Mary Dupuy Smith, M.S. Ed.

Listening Skills for Young Children

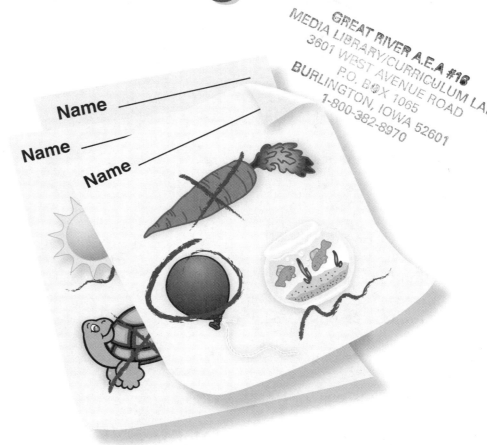

Author

Trish Vowels,

Teacher Created Materials, Inc.
6421 Industry Way
Westminster, CA 92683

www.teachercreated.com

ISBN-0-7439-3264-1

©*2002 Teacher Created Materials, Inc.*
Reprinted, 2002
Made in U.S.A.

Teacher Created Materials

Table of Contents

Introduction

Specific instruction and practice of listening skills prepare a young child for formal learning. As the child develops his or her abilities to focus, interpret, recall, organize, and carry out multiple tasks chronologically, he or she gains confidence and maturity to meet new challenges.

Listening Skills for the Young Child contains teacher-directed activities completed with paper and crayons. These lessons were created as whole-class activities, but may be adapted for use with small groups, individuals, or centers (directed by a parent or aide). There are nine sections: A-H contain 12 lessons each, and Section I contains four lessons. These listening activities begin with simple, single directions and progressively include more complex, multiple directions. In the first section, one direction is given at a time, with the teacher repeating each direction as needed. In the next section, only one direction is given at a time, however, the directions are not repeated until the end of the lesson. In the third section, two directions are given at a time, with repetition as needed. In the fourth section, two directions are given at a time with no repetition of the directions until the end of the lesson. This progression continues throughout the book in order to improve students' listening skills and ability to follow multiple, and increasingly complex, directions.

Due to the simplicity of the activities, answer keys are not provided. You may make keys for the more advanced lessons, if desired.

Also included are teacher-directed physical activities in which children are instructed to move in single or multiple ways. These activities may be completed in the classroom, on the playground or wherever children are grouped. These practices, along with the rhythm clapping suggestions, lend themselves well to getting everyone's attention and bringing a group together.

Included at the beginning of each section are standards of learning, teacher information pertaining to the new skills and how to give directions for that section. Specific directions are set up for teachers, beginning with the word, *say*. It is suggested that these directions be followed as closely as possible. While giving directions, it is important to speak in a calm, slow voice so that children will listen to, remember and follow instructions.

When you foster a fun and challenging learning atmosphere in your classroom, students will strive to listen carefully. Take every opportunity to promote good listening skills. Have students listen for specific details from guest speakers, field trip guides, movies and musical presentations.

Suggestions for Use

Children should be guided step by step through the increasingly complex skills to ensure success at each level. Because each section of activities builds upon the previous section, it is important for children to master each level before moving on to the next. Feel free to do the same lesson repeatedly or the entire section more than once if needed.

If desired, these lessons may be used daily. It is suggested that they be done at least three times per week, especially during the first few sections. Each lesson should take approximately 10-15 minutes.

When beginning Section A, you may wish to start the lessons as a whole-class activity, modeling the lessons for your students as you say the directions aloud. In some sections, directions may be repeated as necessary until the child understands and complies. You may repeat the same page as many times as needed, providing students with practice in concentrated listening. Have extra copies of the activities available for children who become frustrated with their mistakes and want to try again. As students become trained listeners, allow them to be as independent as possible. If a group no longer needs the repetition of directions, even when allowed in the lesson, there is no need to repeat them. However, be sure to monitor students' work and adjust the instruction to their needs.

In some sections, the skill level of difficulty is increased by not repeating instructions after each line of directions. Instead, students have to wait until all directions are given before repetition is allowed. Especially at first, this may cause some frustration. Before you begin a section that follows this procedure, instruct each child to sit quietly until the next direction is given if he or she doesn't remember what to do. Explain that you will go over all of the directions again at the end and the child may catch up then.

At times, children are directed to use a specific crayon color, and sometimes they may choose a color. Pause only a few seconds for them to make this choice. When they are instructed to color quickly, allow a short amount of time (10-15 seconds). Each student should continue to use the same color of crayon until you direct him or her to change colors.

Review the directions of each lesson before you begin, and note which concepts may be new to the students. If needed, you may wish to teach the concept(s) before the lesson. Some examples may be demonstrated during the lesson. For instance, draw a plus sign on the board as you give the direction, "Draw a plus sign above the carrot."

 # Suggestions for Use *(cont.)*

In several lessons, some pictures on the student pages are not used during the listening activity. These pictures are included to increase the difficulty of the exercise. Be aware that many young learners will want to use everything on the page. You may choose to discuss this with your class, explaining that the children can show their good listening skills by ignoring the pictures that are not mentioned.

Some directions tell students "to color quickly." They will need to be assured that you do not expect them to "stay in the lines" or color particularly neatly; they simply need to color the item mentioned. Also, some directions instruct students to color an item an unusual color (such as a blue apple). To prevent students from becoming upset by this, you may wish to forewarn them and stress that they can show they are good listeners by doing exactly what you say.

If you choose to use this book for center activities, be sure that the parent or aide directing the centers has a full understanding of how to give the directions.

In the last section of this book, you will find samples for listening to and following physical directions. These can be done at your convenience for any length of time. Daily participation in these activities has a great effect on sharpening the concentration and listening skills of young children.

How to Give Directions

Nine sections of listening and written activities are included in this book. Review each section's "Teacher Information" beforehand so that you know the new skill(s) that will be introduced. Remember to also look for new concepts that should be covered before or during the lesson. At the beginning of each section, it is necessary to explain to students the procedure for the lessons in that section. You may need to repeat these guidelines for each lesson until the students are comfortable with them. Before beginning formal directions, provide the children with the necessary materials and make sure you have their attention. Remember to consistently reinforce good listening skills by saying phrases such as, "Listen carefully," or "Good listening!"

Think of giving the instructions in a similar manner as administering a standardized test: speak slowly, pause between directions and wander around the room to check students' progress. As a general rule, allow about 10-20 seconds for students to complete one line of directions. You may need to provide more time (about five seconds per task) for the students as the level of difficulty increases.

When a new concept occurs, feel free to demonstrate. For example, the first time you direct students to "Draw a line under the doll," you may need to demonstrate what that means. Specific guidelines are located at the beginning of each section.

Section A

Standards

Student will:

- follow single, oral directions
- recognize colors: red, green, black, orange, blue, pink
- draw shapes: triangle, circle, ring, box
- draw: symbol X, line, squiggly line
- recognize spatial positions: under, above

Teacher Information

In Section A, one direction is given in each line; the teacher may repeat each direction as needed.

Speak slowly and clearly. Repeat the directions as often as needed. Since these are beginning listening activities, you may demonstrate the lessons and provide extra pages for children to re-do. If you choose to do any of these lessons with the children, instruct them to do what you do as you give the directions.

At the beginning of each lesson, say, "We are practicing to be better listeners. I will tell you what to do on your picture page. Listen carefully and then do what I have said. If you need help or forget the directions, wait for me to say them again. Listen carefully, and follow the directions. Ready?"

Directions for Section A Lesson 1, page 10

Say: "Pick up a crayon.

Put your crayon on the teddy bear.

Draw a line from the teddy bear to the ball. (may demonstrate)

Color the flower.

Put down your crayon."

Directions for Section A Lesson 2, page 11

Say: "Pick up a crayon.

Put your crayon on the star.

Draw a line from the star to the doll.

Color the cat quickly.

Put down your crayon."

Directions for Section A Lesson 3, page 12

Say: "Pick up a crayon.

Make a ring around the butterfly. (may demonstrate)

Put your crayon on the snake.

Draw a line from the snake to the lion.

Put down your crayon."

Directions for Section A Lesson 4, page 13

Say: "Pick up a crayon.

Color the shirt quickly.

Make a big X on the book. (may demonstrate)

Draw a line from the book to the strawberry.

Put down your crayon."

Section A (cont.)

Directions for Section A Lesson 5, page 14

Say: "Pick up a red crayon.

Put your crayon on the leaf.

Draw a line from the leaf to the sun.

Color the apple quickly.

Put down your crayon."

Directions for Section A Lesson 6, page 15

Say: "Pick up a green crayon.

Color the fish quickly.

Make a ring around the duck.

Draw a line under the flower. (may demonstrate)

Put down your crayon."

Directions for Section A Lesson 7, page 16

Say: "Pick up a black crayon.

Draw a line under the doll.

Make an X on the hat.

Draw a line from the candy cane to the hat.

Put down your crayon."

Directions for Section A Lesson 8, page 17

Say: "Pick up an orange crayon.

Color the pumpkin quickly.

Make a ring around the birdhouse.

Make a box under the clover. (may demonstrate)

Put down your crayon."

Directions for Section A Lesson 9, page 18

Say: "Pick up a blue crayon.

Draw a line from the umbrella to the Easter egg.

Circle the butterfly. (may demonstrate)

Color the handle on the umbrella.

Put down your crayon."

Directions for Section A Lesson 10, page 19

Say: "Pick up a crayon.

Draw a line under the bird.

Make a triangle around the book. (may demonstrate)

Choose a different crayon.

Make an X on the sun.

Draw a line from the book to the bird.

Put down your crayon."

Directions for Section A Lesson 11, page 20

Say: "Pick up a red crayon.

Color the flag quickly.

Make a triangle around the ball.

Choose a different crayon.

Circle the glasses.

Draw a squiggly line from the ball to the glasses. (may demonstrate)

Put down your crayon."

Directions for Section A Lesson 12, page 21

Say: "Pick up a pink crayon.

Make a big X under the cupcake.

Make a big X above the lamb.

Color the kite quickly.

Choose a different color.

Color the cupcake frosting.

Put down your crayon."

Name _____

Name _____

Section A   **Lesson 2**

Name _____

Name _____

Name _____

Name _____

Section A   **Lesson 9**

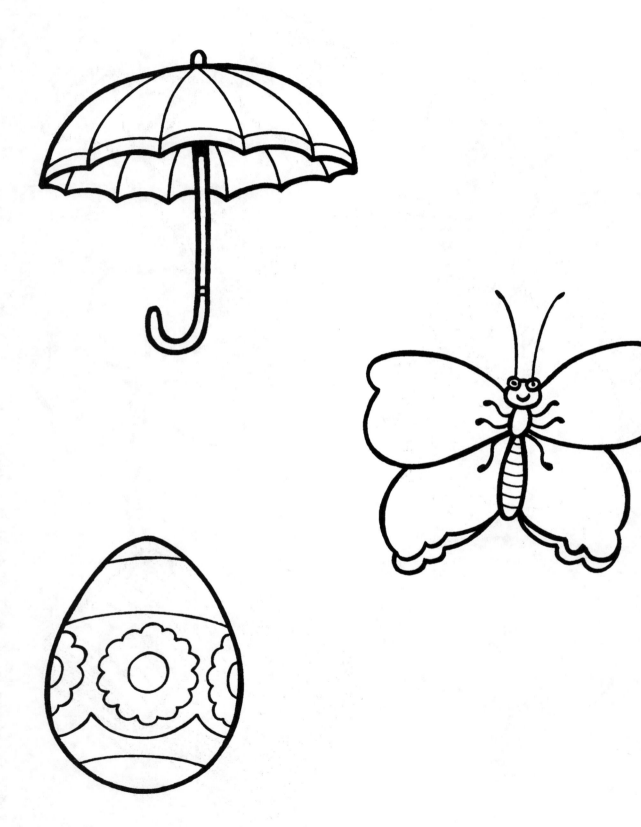

Name _____

Section A

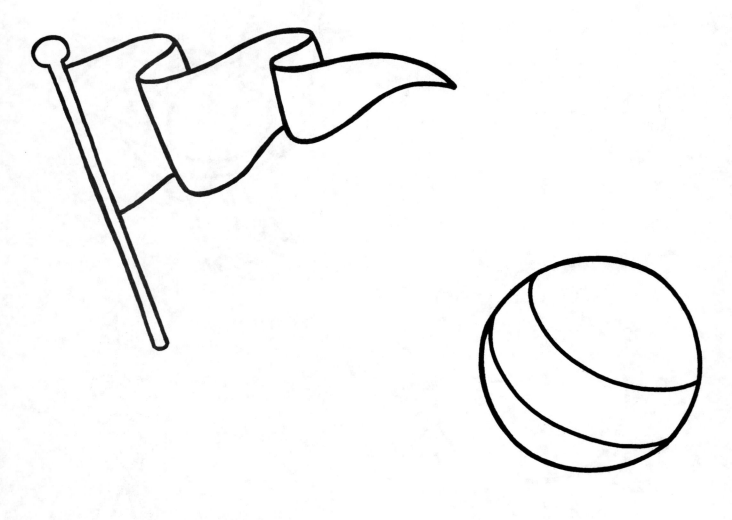

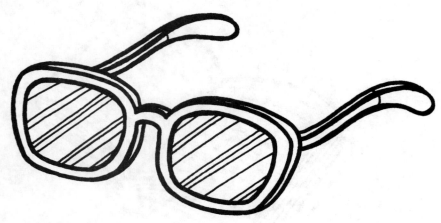

Name _____

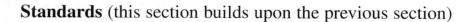

Section B

Standards (this section builds upon the previous section)

Student will:

- follow single, oral directions, not repeated until the end of the lesson
- recognize color: brown
- recognize shape: rectangle
- draw shape: heart
- draw: big dot
- recognize spatial positions: bottom, inside

Teacher Information

In Section B, one direction is given in each line; the teacher may not repeat directions until the end of the lesson.

Explain that you will say what to do only one time until the end of the lesson, at which time you will repeat the directions so that everyone can catch up or check his or her work. Encourage students to try to remember what to do, and if they forget, to sit very quietly and wait for the next direction. This may be frustrating for young children at first; however, with reassurance and practice, this skill will be developed. Allow children to correct or complete their work when you repeat the directions at the end. Praise them for what they did correctly.

At the beginning of each lesson, say, "Listen very carefully because I will tell you what to do only one time. If you forget what to do, skip that part and wait until I tell you the next direction. At the end of the lesson, I will say everything again, and you may catch up or check your work. Ready?"

Directions for Section B Lesson 13, page 26

Say: "Pick up a crayon.

Put your crayon on the ladybug.

Draw a line to the door.

Color the box.

Put down your crayon."

Directions for Section B Lesson 14, page 27

Say: "Pick up a crayon.

Put the crayon on the tree.

Draw a line from the tree to the chair.

Then draw a line from the chair to the ball.

Lastly, draw a line from the ball to the tree."

Directions for Section B Lesson 15, page 28

Say: "Pick up a crayon.

Put the crayon on the big X.

Draw a line from the X to the butterfly.

Next, color the happy face.

Put down your crayon."

Directions for Section B Lesson 16, page 29

Say: "Pick up a crayon.

Make a ring around one of the shirts.

Make a big X on the other shirt.

Put your crayon on the bee.

Draw a line from the bee to the triangle.

Put down your crayon."

Directions for Section B Lesson 17, page 30

Say: "Pick up a black crayon.

Draw a line under the ball.

Color the rectangle quickly.

Make a ring around the cat.

Put down your crayon."

Directions for Section B Lesson 18, page 31

Say: "Pick up a blue crayon.

Put your crayon on the pear.

Draw a line from the pear to the mouse.

Color the bottom part of the boat quickly. (may demonstrate)

Draw a line under the pear.

Put down your crayon."

Directions for Section B Lesson 19, page 32

Say: "Pick up a black crayon.

Make a ring around the shoe.

Make an X on the moon.

Put your crayon on the peanut.

Draw a line from the peanut to the shoe.

Put down your crayon."

Directions for Section B Lesson 20, page 33

Say: "Pick up a crayon.

Color the broom quickly.

Draw a squiggly line under the gingerbread boy.

Make a box around the candle.

Draw a big dot above the broom. (may demonstrate)

Put down your crayon."

Directions for Section B Lesson 21, page 34

Say: "Pick up a green crayon.

Draw a circle inside the triangle. (may demonstrate)

Make an X on the doghouse door.

Choose a different crayon.

Draw a line from the stop sign to the triangle.

Circle the stop sign.

Put down your crayon."

Directions for Section B Lesson 22, page 35

Say: "Pick up an orange crayon.

Make a triangle around the footprint.

Choose a different crayon.

Draw a line under the horn.

Put your crayon on the carrot.

Draw a line from the carrot to the horn.

Put down your crayon."

Directions for Section B Lesson 23, page 36

Say: "Pick up a brown crayon.

Draw a big dot on the dog's ear.

Draw a heart inside of the heart on your page. (may demonstrate)

Choose a green crayon.

Make a ring around the fish.

Make a ring around the dog.

Put down your crayon."

Directions for Section B Lesson 24, page 37

Say: "Pick up a red crayon.

Color the balloon quickly.

Put your crayon on the bee.

Draw a line from the bee to the horse.

Choose a different crayon.

Make a big X under the bee.

Draw a line above the horse.

Put down your crayon."

Name _____

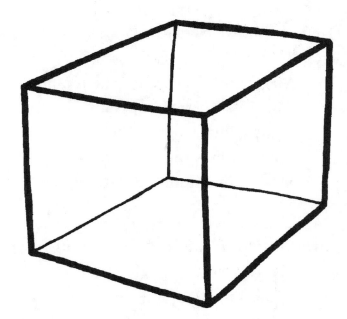

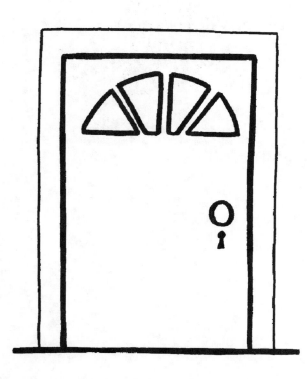

Name _____

Section B   **Lesson 14**

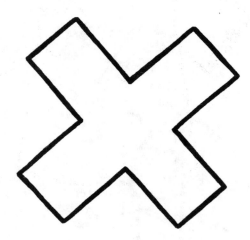

Name _____

Name _____

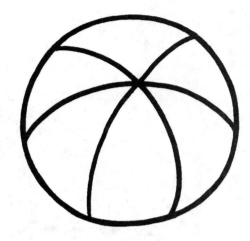

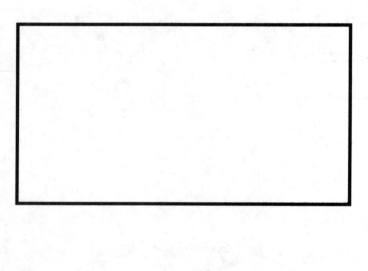

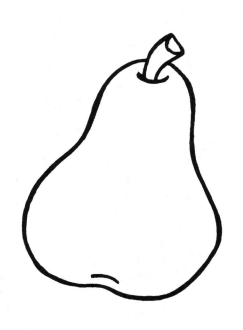

Name _____

Name _____

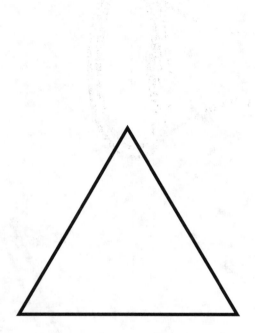

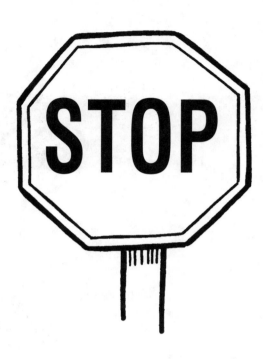

Name _____

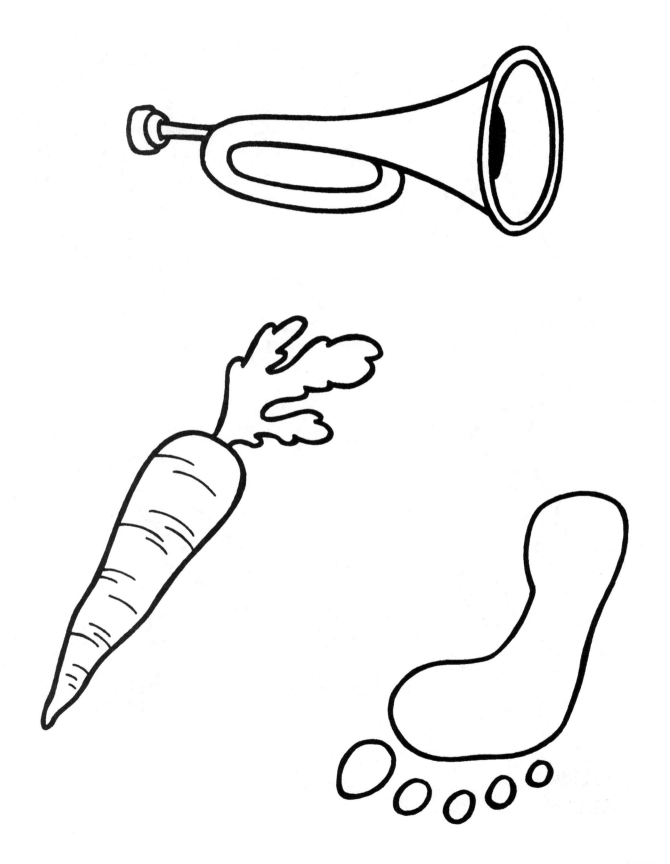

Name _____

Section B   **Lesson 24**

Section C

Standards (this section builds upon the previous section)

Student will:

- follow two oral directions
- recognize color: purple
- understand concept: stripes
- draw symbol: plus sign (+)

Teacher Information

In section C, one or two directions are given in each line; the teacher may repeat each direction as needed.

Children will learn to follow more than one direction in one line of instruction. You may inspire your students by telling them they are now ready to do more than one thing at a time. Speak slowly and pause between directions. You may repeat the line of directions, but pause before doing so to give students time to comply. Remind students that some pictures will not be used on their picture pages.

Before each lesson, say, "Listen carefully because I will tell you to do more than one thing. If you forget what to do, sit quietly and wait for me to give the direction again. At the end of the lesson, I will say everything again, and you may finish or check your work. Try your best to listen carefully and follow the directions. Ready?"

Directions for Section C Lesson 25, page 42

Say: "Pick up a blue crayon and draw a line from the bird to the purse.

Put down the blue crayon.

Pick up a red crayon and draw a line from the kite to the flower.

Using the red crayon, circle the bird.

Put down the red crayon."

Directions for Section C Lesson 26, page 43

Say: "Pick up a red crayon.

Circle the house and color the happy face.

Put down the red crayon and pick up a green crayon.

Draw a line from the mouse to the happy face, and put down the green crayon."

Directions for Section C Lesson 27, page 44

Say: "Pick up a crayon and color the clock.

Choose a new crayon and circle the pillow.

Choose another crayon and draw a line from the boy to the ice-cream cone.

Make a big X over the glass.

Put down your crayon."

Directions for Section C Lesson 28, page 45

Say: "Pick up a green crayon and circle the mouse.

Choose a new crayon and color the moon.

Draw a line from the moon to the mouse; then draw a line under the umbrella.

Put down your crayon."

Directions for Section C Lesson 29, page 46

Say: "Pick up a crayon and color the turtle's shell.

Draw a line under the turtle and make an X on the birdhouse.

Color the hat and put down the crayon."

Directions for Section C Lesson 30, page 47

Say: "Pick up a red crayon.

Color the watermelon red and make an X below the flower.

Pick up a blue crayon and draw a line from the cow to the watermelon.

Put down the blue crayon."

Directions for Section C Lesson 31, page 48

Say: "Choose a crayon and color the fish in the bowl.

Draw a line from the carrot to the balloon; and then draw a line from the balloon to the fishbowl.

Pick up a green crayon and color the leaf on the carrot.

Put down your crayon."

Directions for Section C Lesson 32, page 49

Say: "Pick up a brown crayon.

Make an X inside the heart and an X inside the acorn.

Choose a new crayon and draw a line under the fish.

Color the moon and make a ring around it.

Put down your crayon."

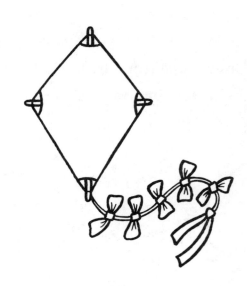

Directions for Section C Lesson 33, page 50

Say: "Pick up a red crayon and color the bell.

Make an X on the cloud and color the stripes on the candy cane. (may demonstrate)

Make a ring around the pumpkin and draw a line from the pumpkin to the candy cane.

Put down your crayon."

Directions for Section C Lesson 34, page 51

Say: "Choose a crayon and draw a line from the flower to the bunny.

Circle the flower and draw a + (plus sign) inside the sun. (may demonstrate)

Draw a line under the clock and put down your crayon."

Directions for Section C Lesson 35, page 52

Say: "Pick up a black crayon and make a big X on the strawberry.

Draw a line from the bug to the butterfly and then from the butterfly to the rooster.

Put down your crayon."

Directions for Section C Lesson 36, page 53

Say: "Pick up a purple crayon and make a ring around the cupcake.

Draw a line from the cupcake to the hat and color the button quickly.

Draw a plus sign above the ribbon and a line under the hat.

Put down your crayon."

Name _____

Section C   **Lesson 26**

Name _____

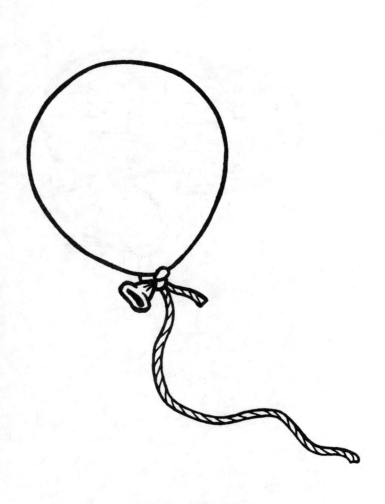

Name _____

Name _____

Section C

Name _____

Standards (this section builds upon the previous section)

Student will:

- follow two oral directions, not repeated until the end of the lesson
- recognize shapes: square, diamond
- recognize numeral: 5
- compare size: big, little

Teacher Information

In section D, one or two directions are given in each line; the teacher may not repeat the directions until the end of the lesson.

In this section, children will continue to follow more than one direction. However, they will do so without any repetition of directions until the end of the lesson. Discuss this procedure with them, and assure students that if they forget a step, they should wait for you to say the next direction. Explain that you will say everything again at the end of the lesson and they may catch up then.

At the beginning of each lesson, say, "We will continue practicing to follow more than one direction, but now I will not repeat each line. I will wait until the end of the lesson before I say the directions again. You need to listen very carefully and try to remember what to do. If you forget, wait quietly until I give the next direction. When I repeat the instructions at the end, you may finish or check your work. Ready?"

Directions for Section D Lesson 37, page 58

Say: "Pick up a brown crayon and circle the clock.

Make an X on the acorn, and draw a line under the mouse.

Pick up a green crayon and draw a line from the hat to the happy face.

Put down your crayon."

Directions for Section D Lesson 38, page 59

Say: "Pick up a pink crayon, and color the cupcake quickly.

Draw a line from the turtle to the button, and then draw a line from the button to the strawberry.

Pick up an orange crayon, and circle the cloud.

Draw a line under the turtle and put down your crayon."

Directions for Section D Lesson 39, page 60

Say: "Choose a crayon and draw a line from the fish to the triangle.

Color the moon quickly and make an X on the pear.

Choose another crayon and circle the cap.

Draw a plus sign under the fish and put down your crayon." (May demonstrate)

Directions for Section D Lesson 40, page 61

Say: "Pick up a red crayon and draw a big dot inside the apple.

Make an X inside the heart and draw a line under the light bulb.

Pick up a blue crayon and color the raindrop quickly.

Draw a line from the flower to the light bulb and put down your crayon."

Directions for Section D Lesson 41, page 62

Say: "Choose a crayon and make a circle around the square.

Draw a line from the bucket to the ice-cream cone, and then draw a line from the star to the leaf.

Draw a big dot inside the star and a plus sign inside the square.

Put down your crayon."

Directions for Section D Lesson 42, page 63

Say: "Pick up a blue crayon and color the lollipop quickly.

Circle the diamond and then make a box around the banana.

Pick up a green crayon and make a big X above the sun.

Draw a line under the lollipop and put down your crayon."

Directions for Section D Lesson 43, page 64

Say: "Choose a crayon and draw a plus sign inside the big circle. (may demonstrate)

Draw a line from the drum to the little circle, and then draw a line from the little circle to the glass.

Make an X above the cake and another X under the cake.

Put down your crayon."

Directions for Section D Lesson 44, page 65

Say: "Pick up a red crayon, and make a ring around the bowl.

Draw a big dot inside the arrow and draw a line from the pumpkin to the kite.

Pick up a blue crayon, and make a box around the bug.

Put down your crayon."

Directions for Section D Lesson 45, page 66

Say: "Pick up a black crayon and color the key quickly.

Pick up a green crayon and make a big X on the tree.

Draw a line from the key to the wheel, and then draw a line from the brush to the butterfly.

Draw a line under the key, and put down your crayon."

Directions for Section D Lesson 46, page 67

Say: "Choose a crayon and circle the stool.

Make an X below the ring and an X above the eye.

Choose a different crayon and draw a line from the lamp to the present.

Draw a plus sign above the stool and put down your crayon."

Directions for Section D Lesson 47, page 68

Say: "Pick up a brown crayon and draw a line from the snail to the scissors.

Pick up a green crayon and draw a squiggly line from the sad face to the snail.

Circle the happy face and make a box around the scissors.
Make an X above the snake and put down your crayon."

Directions for Section D Lesson 48, page 69

Say: "Choose a crayon and make a box around the numeral 5.

Circle the plus sign and draw a line from the fish to the rectangle.

Choose a different crayon and color the fish quickly.

Draw a line under the horse and put down your crayon."

Name _____

Name _____

Section D   **Lesson 40**

Name _____

Name _____

Name _____

Name _____

Section D   **Lesson 48**

5

+

Section E

Standards (this section builds upon the previous section)

Student will:

- follow three oral directions, listening to one entire line of directions before beginning
- recognize color: yellow
- understand concept: copy over
- draw: happy face

Teacher Information

In section E, multiple directions are given in each line (choosing a crayon counts as a direction). Furthermore, the children must not begin to work until one entire line of directions is given. The teacher may repeat each direction as needed.

In Section E, multiple directions are continued, but the activity is more difficult because children must not begin to follow directions until one entire line of directions is given. This encourages them to listen more intently and remember more. After each line, you may pause and repeat the directions as needed. However, as students' listening skills develop, attempt to do less repeating. You should end every line of instructions with the word, *now*, as this will be their cue to begin to follow the directions. This procedure should be thoroughly explained, and perhaps practiced, before beginning. Since this is a higher skill, you may wish to model or repeat the lessons until the children are comfortable with them.

At the beginning of each lesson, say, "We will keep listening as we have been, but now you should not begin working until I finish giving the direction. At the end of the direction, I will say, *now*, and that will be the signal for you to start. You need to listen closely and try to remember what to do. I will repeat the directions if you need me to, but do your best to do everything correctly the first time. You will need to listen very carefully. Ready?"

Directions for Section E Lesson 49, page 74

Say: "Make an X inside the circle with a blue crayon – now.

Draw a circle inside the square and another circle around the square – now.

Color the truck with two colors – now.

Put down your crayon – now."

Directions for Section E Lesson 50, page 75

Say: "Draw a line under the bug with a red crayon – now.

Circle the ball and circle the kite with a purple crayon – now.

Put down your crayon – now."

Directions for Section E Lesson 51, page 76

Say: "Make a blue box around the teddy bear – now.

Draw a red line under the paintbrush and a red circle around the tree – now.

Put down your crayon – now."

Directions for Section E Lesson 52, page 77

Say: "Color the heart red and color the cap green – now.

Make a blue circle around the rocket and a blue line under the doghouse – now.

Put down your crayon – now."

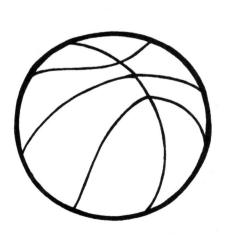

Directions for Section E Lesson 53, page 78

Say: "Put your orange crayon on the spoon, and draw a line to the apple – now.

Put your orange crayon on the whale and draw a squiggly line to the owl – now.

Color one of the pictures blue; then put down your crayon – now."

Directions for Section E Lesson 54, page 79

Say: "Quickly color the bunny black and the circle yellow – now.

Make a big red ring, with the bow, the kitten and the raindrop inside – now.

Put down your crayon – now."

Directions for Section E Lesson 55, page 80

Say: "Draw a black line under the flower and a black line above the moon – now.

Draw a brown line from the stop sign to the bird, and then to the cloud – now.

Put down your crayon – now."

Directions for Section E Lesson 56, page 81

Say: "Choose a crayon and circle the apple – now.

Draw a line from the snowman to the fish and then from the star to the snail – now.

Color the hat on the snowman, and color the leaf on the apple – now.

Put down your crayon – now."

Section E (cont.)

Directions for Section E Lesson 57, page 82

Say: "Pick up an orange crayon and draw a plus sign inside the egg – now.

Draw a line under the bucket and make an X above the moon – now.

Make a ring around the bird, and draw a line from the bird to the flower – now.

Put down your crayon – now."

Directions for Section E Lesson 58, page 83

Say: "Pick up a red crayon and draw a line from the happy face to the heart – now.

Make an X inside the heart and copy over the smile on the happy face – now. (may demonstrate)

Using a black crayon, draw a circle inside the rectangle – now.

Draw a squiggly line from the pig to the barn, and put down your crayon – now."

Directions for Section E Lesson 59, page 84

Say: "Pick up a blue crayon and color the birthday hat quickly – now.

Using a red crayon, color the cherry on the ice-cream cone and make a ring around the pitcher – now.

Draw a line from the balloon to the ice-cream cone, and then make a line from the ice-cream cone to the bee – now.

Put down your crayon – now."

Directions for Section E Lesson 60, page 85

Say: "With a green crayon, make one big box with the cup and leaf inside – now.

With a brown crayon, draw a line from the candle to the pear, and then from the pear to the stocking – now.

Make an X under the candle and a ring around the pear – now.

Draw a happy face under your name, and put down your crayon – now." (may demonstrate)

Name _____

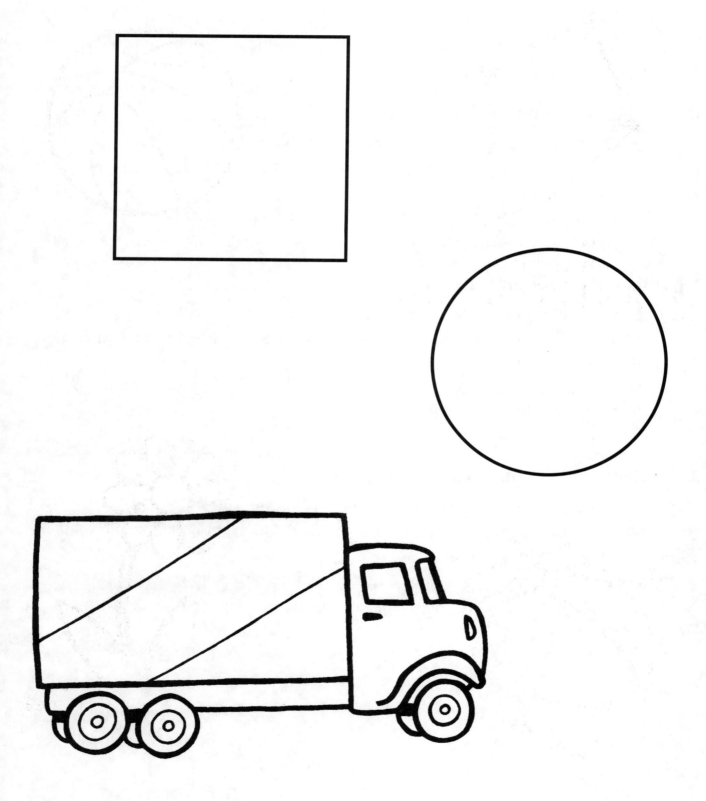

Name _____

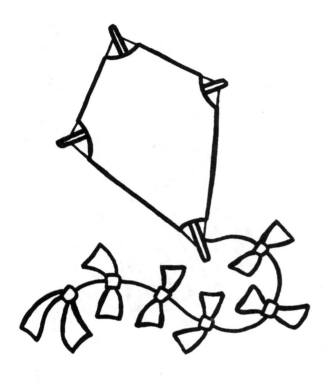

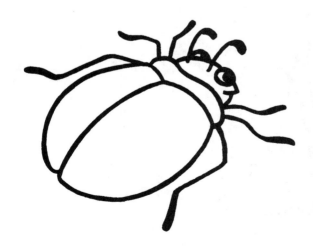

Name _____

Name _____

Name _____

Section E   **Lesson 54**

Name _____

Name _____

Name _____

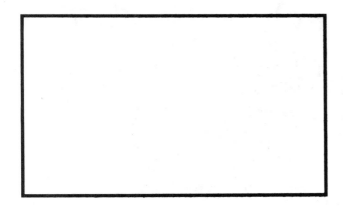

Name _____

Name _____

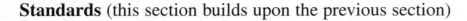

Standards (this section builds upon the previous section)

Student will:

- follow three oral directions, not repeated until the end of the lesson

Teacher Information

In Section F, students will continue to follow multiple directions in a line before beginning to work. The directions will not be repeated, however, until the very end of the lesson. Students should be reminded, again, that if they forget what to do, they should wait quietly for you to give the next direction. Assure them that you will give all of the directions at the end and they may catch up then. As with all of the sections, children may repeat certain lessons or the entire section, if needed, before advancing to the next level.

Before beginning each lesson, say, "You will continue following all of the directions I give after you hear the word, *now*. I will not tell you them again until we finish the page. If you forget what I have said, skip the part that you don't remember. Then sit quietly until I give the next instruction. I will say everything again at the end, and you may catch up or fix anything that isn't correct. Listen carefully, and when I say, *now*, you may begin. Ready?"

Section F (cont.)

Directions for Section F Lesson 61, page 90

Say: "Color the raindrop blue, and make a red ring around the kitten – now.

Make a blue X inside the egg, and draw a line from the egg to the drum – now.

Draw a green line under the pencil, and put down your crayon – now."

Directions for Section F Lesson 62, page 91

Say: "Make a black X inside the big box and a red X inside the little box – now.

Draw a green line from the triangle to the bone and from the bone to the cake – now.

Make a red ring around the cake, and put down your crayon – now."

Directions for Section F Lesson 63, page 92

Say: "Color the star yellow and the glass of juice orange – now.

Make one big ring with the umbrella and the flower inside – now.

Make a brown X under the bat, and put down your crayon – now."

Directions for Section F Lesson 64, page 93

Say: "Draw a black plus sign inside the acorn and a red plus sign under the acorn – now.

Color the shorts blue, and color the ball orange – now.

Draw a green line from the butterfly to the ball, and put down your crayon – now."

Section F (cont.)

Directions for Section F Lesson 65, page 94

Say: "Using a red crayon, color the lollipop, and make a ring around the cupcake – now.

Using a green crayon, make a big X on the tree, and draw a line from the tree to the light bulb – now.

Using a yellow crayon, color the arrow, and then put down your crayon – now."

Directions for Section F Lesson 66, page 95

Say: "Color the smile on the jack-o-lantern and the shovel red – now.

Make a blue ring around the moon and a green X on the cloud – now.

Color two stripes on the hat black and make a black line from the hat to the cloud – now.

Put down your crayon – now."

Directions for Section F Lesson 67, page 96

Say: "Color the diamond blue and the apple red – now.

Make one brown ring around the table and paintbrush, with both inside – now.

Draw a green line from the apple to the bowl, and put down your crayon – now."

Directions for Section F Lesson 68, page 97

Say: "Color the flower pink, and color the bug red – now.

Make a red ring around the knife, and draw a line from the knife to the ball – now.

Color the stripe on the ball yellow, and put down your crayon – now."

Directions for Section F Lesson 69, page 98

Say: "Draw a line from the flag to the turtle to the banana with a blue crayon – now.

Draw a green line under the wheel and a purple line above the flag – now.

Using a black crayon, make a ring around the banana, and put down your crayon – now."

Directions for Section F Lesson 70, page 99

Say: "Draw a red line above the paper clip, and color the tree trunk brown – now.

Draw a blue line from the candle to the tree, going under the paper clip – now.

Color the fish orange, and draw a black line under it – now.

Put down your crayon – now."

Directions for Section F Lesson 71, page 100

Say: "Draw a brown line from the butterfly to the star to the cup – now.

Draw a plus sign on the steps using your red crayon, and make a blue ring around the man – now.

Color the cup pink, and draw a big yellow dot inside the star – now.

Put down your crayon – now."

Directions for Section F Lesson 72, page 101

Say: "Make a purple box around the key, and draw a red circle inside the rectangle – now.

Draw a green line from the doghouse to the comb to the elephant – now.

Using a blue crayon, draw a line under the comb and make an X on the elephant – now.

Put down your crayon – now."

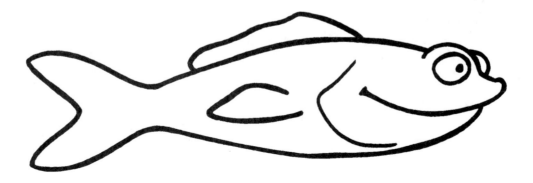

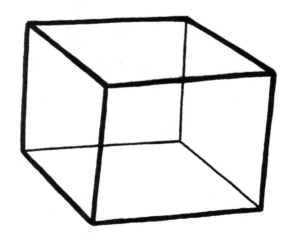

Section F   **Lesson 63**

Name _____

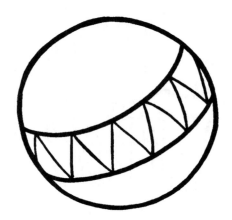

Name _____

Section F   **Lesson 67**

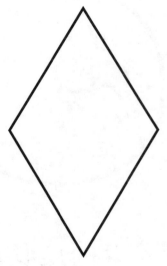

Name _____

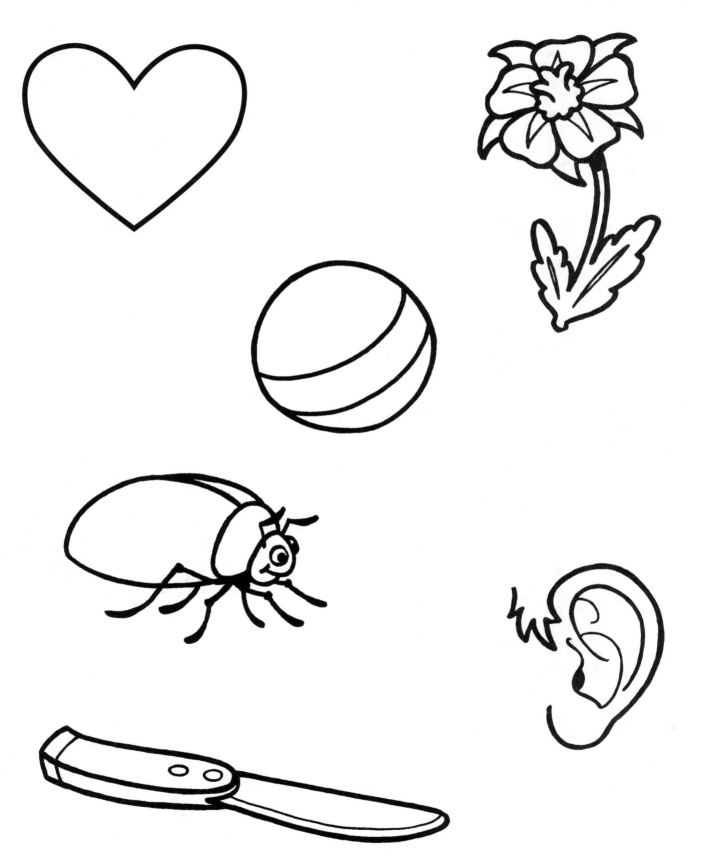

Section F

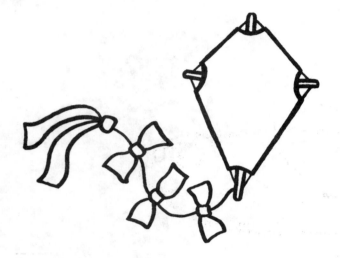

Name _____

Name _____

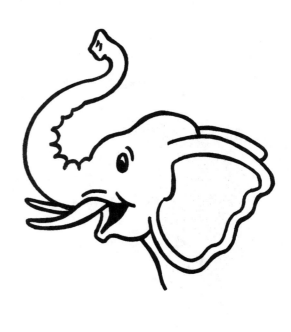

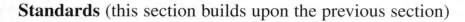

Section G

Standards (this section builds upon the previous section)

Student will:

- follow multiple directions (choosing a crayon color is considered a task)
- understand concept: empty space
- draw: sun
- recognize spatial positions: next to, middle, top
- compare height: short, tall

Teacher Information

In Section G, multiple directions are given, and students must wait for the cue to begin each task. The teacher may repeat each line of direction as needed.

Students will continue the same pattern of listening and following directions, but there will be more tasks to remember in each line. Remember to speak slowly and pause slightly between directions. Students should wait for your cue of the word, *now*, before starting to work. You may repeat each line of directions, however, pause to allow them to have a chance to succeed without repetition.

The last six lessons in Section G are set up differently than lessons included in the previous sections; the student page contains three pictures and three empty spaces. Take time to explain to students that they will use the pictures and empty spaces to complete each activity. You may wish to model the first lesson for your students.

At the beginning of each lesson, say, "Listen carefully to what I say, and wait for me to say the word, *now*, before you begin to work on your page. If you forget a direction, just sit quietly, and I will repeat the direction again. I will tell you the directions as many times as you need. Ready?"

Directions for Section G Lesson 73, page 106

Say: "Make a blue box around the umbrella, and a green circle around the pillow; then draw a purple line under the eye – now.

Color the sun yellow and the ice cream pink; then put down your crayon – now."

Directions for Section G Lesson 74, page 107

Say: "Color the basket red, color the key green and color the present yellow – now.

Make a blue ring around the present, the tree and the basket, with all three inside – now.

Put down your crayon – now."

Directions for Section G Lesson 75, page 108

Say: "Put your black crayon on the flower, and draw a line from the flower to the cactus, going under the kite – now.

Put your red crayon on the tall stickman, and draw a line from it to the short stickman, going above the kite – now.

Color the stool yellow and the cactus brown, and put down your crayon – now."

Directions for Section G Lesson 76, page 109

Say: "Draw a black dot inside the box and a black circle inside the heart – now.

Draw a green line from the lamp to the box to the chair – now.

Draw an orange line from the flag to the heart to the star – now.

Put down your crayon – now."

Directions for Section G Lesson 77, page 110

Say: "Using a blue crayon, draw a line from the ring to the ice-cream cone to the sad face – now.

Color the flashlight red, the ice cream pink and the ring yellow – now.

Put down your crayon – now."

Directions for Section G Lesson 78, page 111

Say: "Using a green crayon, make a big ring with the vase, the car and the triangle inside – now.

Using a black crayon, draw a line from the fork to the snake going around the square – now.

Color the square, the triangle and the fork orange – now.

Put down your crayon – now."

Directions for Section G Lesson 79, page 112

Say: "Using a green crayon, circle the scissors and draw a square in the empty space next to the airplane – now. (may demonstrate)
Using a black crayon, draw a line under the plane and draw a happy face in the space next to the apple – now.

Color the apple red, and draw a triangle in the space next to the scissors – now.

Put down your crayon – now."

Directions for Section G Lesson 80, page 113

Say: "Color the leaf green, and make a red circle around the kitten – now.

Make a brown X in the space next to the kitten, and color the bucket blue – now.

Draw a red triangle in the top space and a blue plus sign in the space next to the leaf – now. (may demonstrate)

Put down your crayon – now."

Directions for Section G Lesson 81, page 114

Say: "Draw a blue happy face in the middle space, next to the sad face, and color the pear yellow – now. (may demonstrate)

Color the ice cream pink and the cone brown, and draw a red cherry in the space next to the ice-cream cone – now.

Make a green X in the space next to the pear, and put down your crayon – now."

Directions for Section G Lesson 82, page 115

Say: "Draw a black triangle in the space next to the ball, and draw a line under the bug using a red crayon – now.

Using a blue crayon, draw a plus sign on the ball and a triangle in the top space next to the bug – now.

Color the triangle under the bug green, and draw a green line from the black triangle to the green triangle to the blue triangle – now.

Put down your crayon – now."

Directions for Section G Lesson 83, page 116

Say: "Draw a big red circle in the space next to the cap and a big blue circle in the space next to the bowl – now.

Color the bowl green, and draw a brown dot inside the red circle – now.

Using a yellow crayon, draw a line above the cap, draw a sun in the space next to the moon, and color the moon – now. (may demonstrate)

Put down your crayon – now."

Directions for Section G Lesson 84, page 117

Say: "Draw a black square in the space next to the owl and make a red X inside the heart – now.

Using a brown crayon, draw a circle in the space next to the heart, a triangle in the space next to the snail, and color the owl – now.

Put down your crayon – now."

Section G   **Lesson 73**

Name _____

Name _____

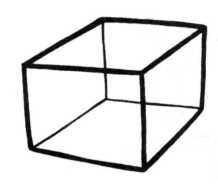

Section G

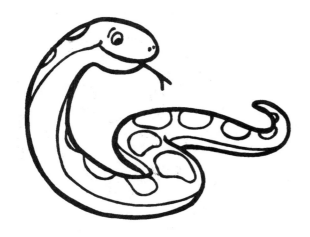

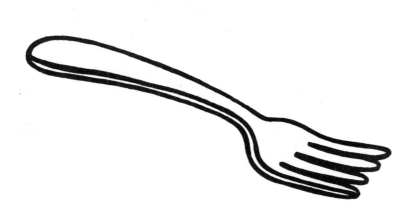

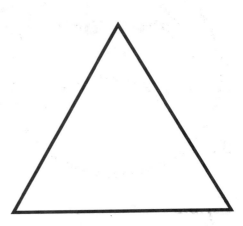

Name _____

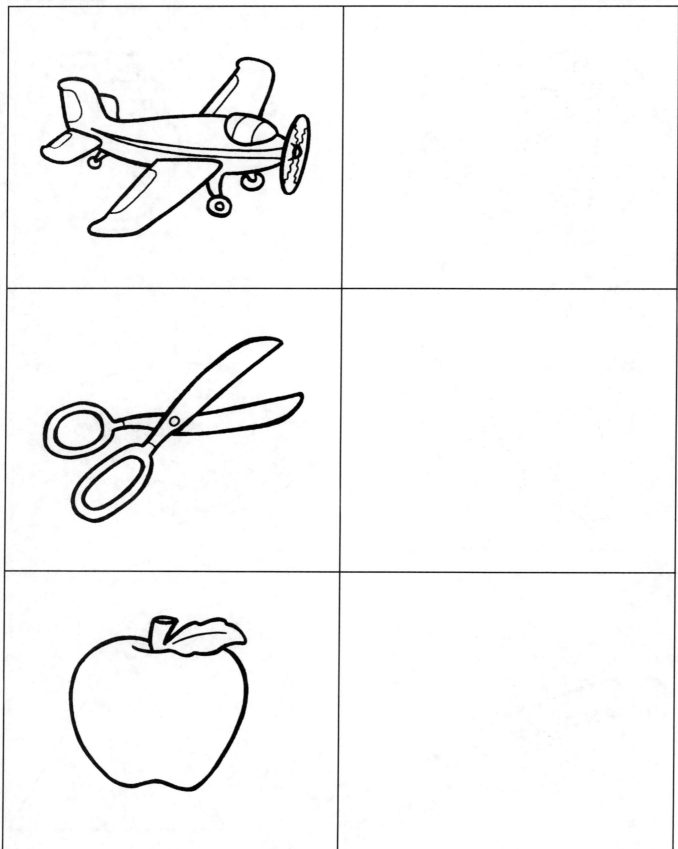

Name _____

Section G

Name _____

Name _____

Name _____

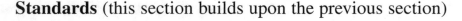

Section H

Standards (this section builds upon the previous section)

Student will:

- follow multiple directions, not repeated until the end of the lesson (choosing a crayon color is considered a task)
- recognize shape: oval
- recognize numerals: 1, 3, 7
- write numerals: 1, 3, 7

Teacher Information

In section H, multiple directions are given in each line, with the choice of crayon color considered as one of the tasks.

The teacher may not repeat a line of directions until the end of the lesson. The student must listen to one entire line of directions before beginning to work. You should end every line of directions with the word, *now*, as this will be the students' cue to begin to work. Discuss with your students the setup of the lessons: the first six pages only have pictures, and the last six have three pictures and three empty spaces.

This section is completed in the same way as the previous section, except that directions are not repeated until the end of the lesson. Again, children should be reminded to sit quietly and wait for the next direction if they don't know what to do. Assure them that they may skip what they forget, and fix anything at the end when you repeat the directions. Also, remind students to wait for your cue of the word, *now*, before they begin to work.

Before beginning each lesson, say, "We are going to do the same kind of listening practice we have been doing, but now we will try to remember what to do without the teacher saying it again. I will only tell you what to do one time, so listen very carefully. At the end of the lesson, I will say everything again, and you may fix anything you forgot. It's okay to skip a step if you forget; just wait quietly for me to give the next direction. Try your best to listen and remember what to do. You may begin when I say the word, *now*. Ready?"

Directions for Section H Lesson 85, page 122

Say: "Using a red crayon, make a big ring with the flower and heart inside – now. Make an X inside the star, draw a big dot inside the heart, and draw a line under the bone – now.

Draw a line from the flower to the star to the numeral 3, and put down your crayon – now."

Directions for Section H Lesson 86, page 123

Say: "Color the big circle blue and the small circle green – now. Draw a red plus sign inside the triangle, and draw a line from the paintbrush to the flower – now. Circle the numeral 7, make an X under the flower, and put down your crayon – now."

Directions for Section H Lesson 87, page 124

Say: "Draw a purple line from the cherry to the orange and a black line from the banana to the cherry – now.

Using a red crayon, make an X inside the rectangle, and color the triangle – now.

Make a blue triangle around the square, and put down your crayon – now."

Directions for Section H Lesson 88, page 125

Say: "Color the balloon yellow, and make a brown circle around the cat – now.

Draw a green line from the kite to the cake and a black line from the star to the cat – now.

Draw a line under the cake and ice-cream cone using red, and put down your crayon – now."

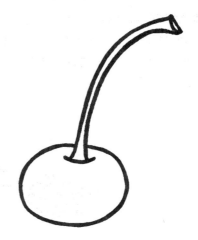

Directions for Section H Lesson 89, page 126

Say: "Make a blue X inside the oval and draw an orange plus sign inside the box – now. (may demonstrate)

Make a big ring around the bear, the spoon and the apple, with all inside – now.

Using a black crayon, draw a line under the box and under the oval – now.

Put down your crayon – now."

Directions for Section H Lesson 90, page 127

Say: "Make a circle around the bird and a box around the umbrella with a black crayon – now.

Make a blue X inside the big circle and a green X inside the little circle – now.

Draw a red line from the pencil to the bird, and put down your crayon – now."

Directions for Section H Lesson 91, page 128

Say: "Color the sun yellow and the diamond red quickly – now.

Draw a circle in the space next to the flag and a triangle next to the sun using blue – now.

Color the circle you drew, and draw a plus sign next to the diamond using green – now.

Put down your crayon – now."

Directions for Section H Lesson 92, page 129

Say: "Using brown, draw a happy face next to the doll and a square next to the star – now.

Make an orange X above the pumpkin, and draw a line under the star using green – now.

Draw a red dot inside the star and in the empty space, and put down your crayon – now."

Directions for Section H Lesson 93, page 130

Say: "Circle the pear, and draw a triangle in the space next to it using blue – now.

Write a black 3 in the space next to the balloon and a red 1 inside the balloon – now. (may demonstrate)

Draw a green square in the empty space, and put down your crayon – now."

Directions for Section H Lesson 94, page 131

Say: "Using a purple crayon, draw a triangle in the middle space and a circle in the top space – now.

Draw a line from the ball to the triangle, and circle the bird – now.

Draw a red square with a circle around it in the empty space, and put down your crayon – now."

Directions for Section H Lesson 95, page 132

Say: "Draw a black line from the flower to the middle space and from the birdhouse to the middle space – now.

Using a green crayon, color the hat quickly, and draw a plus sign in the bottom space – now.

Draw a line under the flower, circle the hat, and put down your crayon – now."

Directions for Section H Lesson 96, page 133

Say: "Using a pink crayon, draw a line from the cupcake to the candy cane – now.

Draw a purple circle in the space next to the umbrella, draw a line under the cup-cake, and make an X in the middle space – now.

Draw a green triangle in the empty space, and put down your crayon – now."

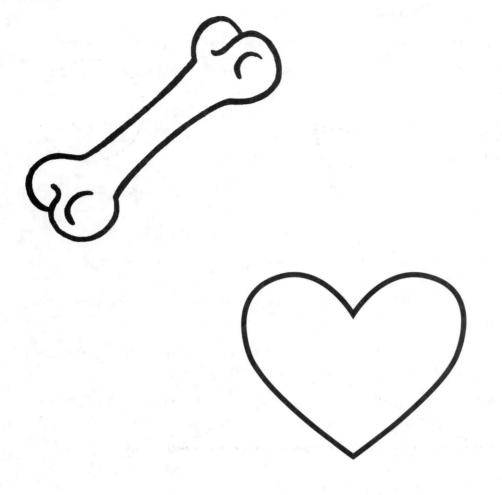

3

7

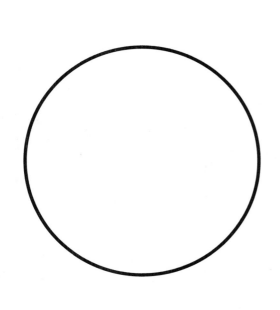

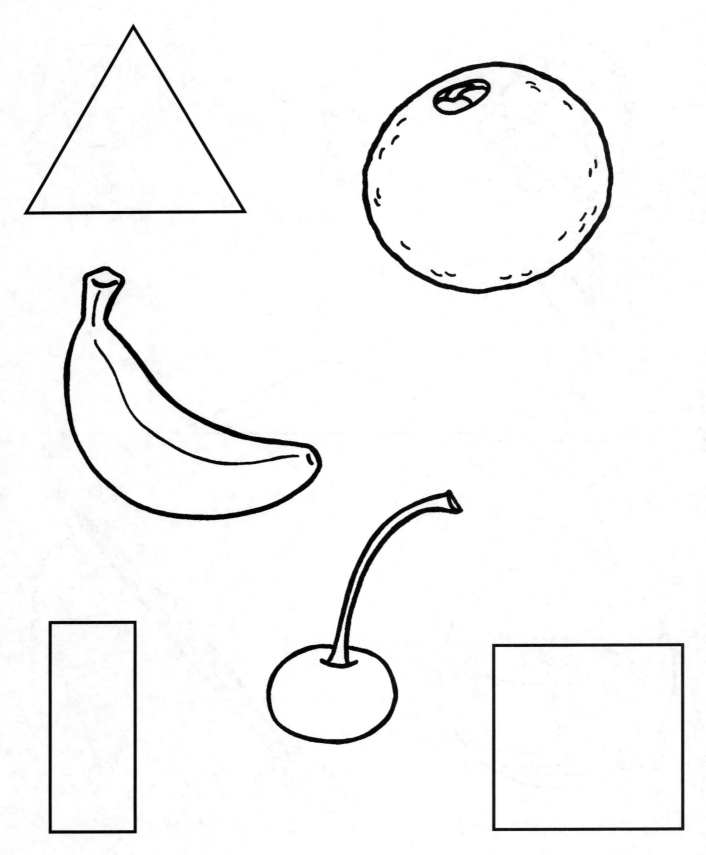

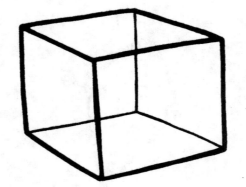

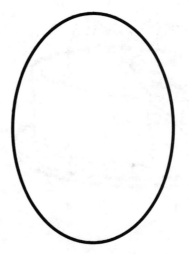

Name _____

Section H

Name _____

Name _____

Name ______________________________

Section H **Lesson 96**

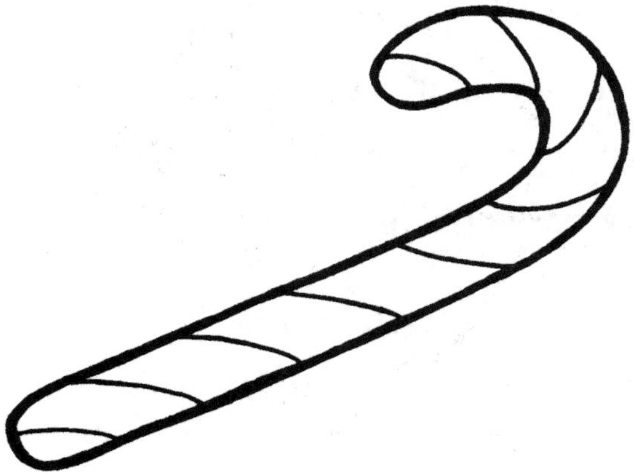

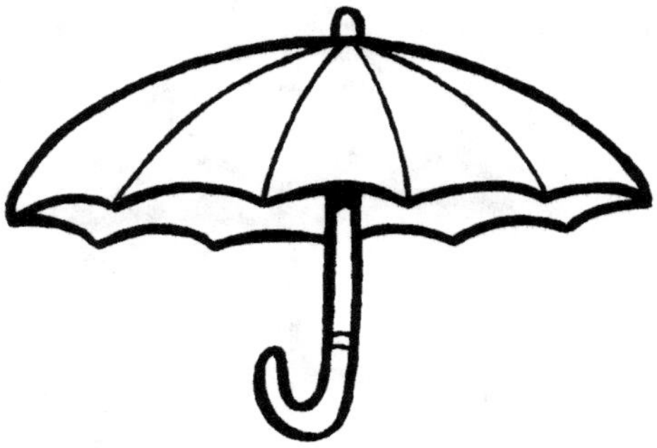

Section I

Standards (this section builds upon the previous section)

Student will:

- follow multiple directions without picture cues
- recognize numerals: 2, 4, 6
- write numerals: 2, 4, 6

Teacher Information

In Section I, multiple directions are given in each line. The student must wait for one entire line of directions to be read before beginning; the teacher will give the cue of the word, *now*, to alert students to begin the task. Children will complete activities composed of six numbered spaces (there are no picture cues). The teacher may repeat the directions as needed.

This is the most advanced listening skill practice included in the book. Students successfully reaching this section should be highly praised. The setup in Section I is different—there are numbered spaces instead of picture cues. Explain to the children that they will be using the numbered spaces to complete tasks as you direct. Continue to remind them of the same rules: wait for the cue word, *now*, and sit quietly while waiting for further directions or repetition if needed. Encourage children to see how often they can complete a line of tasks without repetition of the directions. Later, you may wish for students to complete this section with no repetition to practice a more advanced skill.

Before each lesson, say, "You will see that your page has numbered spaces on it: 1–6 (count these aloud with your students). I will tell you what to do in these spaces. Listen carefully, and see how well you can follow the directions. If you forget, sit quietly and wait for me to repeat the directions. When I say *now*, you may begin. Ready?"

Directions for Section I Lesson 97, page 136

Say: "Pick up a crayon, and draw a circle in space 4 and a line in space 1 – now.

Choose a new crayon, and draw a square in space 5 and a big dot in space 2 – now.

Choose a different crayon, and draw a happy face in space 6, and put down your crayon – now."

Directions for Section I Lesson 98, page 137

Say: "Using a black crayon, draw a square in space 4 and a circle in space 1 – now.

Draw a big dot in space 6 and space 2 using a blue crayon – now.

Draw a red line from the circle to the square to space 5 – now.

In space 3, draw a triangle, and put down your crayon – now."

Directions for Section I Lesson 99, page 138

Say: "In each of spaces 1, 4 and 6, draw a blue circle – now.

Draw a red plus sign in space 3 and a green square in space 5 – now.

Color the circle in space 4 blue, write a purple 6 in space 2, and put down your crayon – now." (may demonstrate)

Directions for Section I Lesson 100, page 139

Say: "Write a yellow 4 in space 2 and a green 2 in space 5 – now. (may demonstrate)

Using a red crayon, make an X in spaces 6, 1 and 3 – now.

Draw a brown happy face in space 4, and draw a line to connect the three X's – now.

Put down your crayon – now."

Name _____

1	2
3	4
5	6